COLUMBUS
In The Bay of Pigs

Family Life.
(From Amerigo Vespucci, *Letter*, 1509)

OTHER BOOKS BY THE AUTHOR

Poetry

Decade: The1990s
Tidal News
Cosmic Athletics
Ride the Wind

History

Work Cooperation in America
Collectivity in the San Francisco Area

❧ Cover illustration from Theodore de Bry, *America*, 1596
❧ Illustration on page 7: Taínos in a canoe, from G. Benzoni, *Historia del Mundo Nuevo*, 1572

COLUMBUS
In The Bay of Pigs

John Curl

HOMEWARD PRESS

ACKNOWLEDGMENTS

Design: Mara Hancock
Printing: Inkworks Press
Project coordination: Inkworks Publishing Committee
Logo: Mayan glyph for solar eclipse drawn by Nancy Gorrell
Design Contributions: Peter Veilleux

Illustrations courtesy of the New York
Public Library Picture Collection.

The quotes in the poem are, in some
instances, composite and condensed.
The originals can be found in the works
cited in the bibliography.

Published by:
HOMEWARD PRESS
P.O. Box 2307
Berkeley, CA 94702

Co-publisher:
INKWORKS PRESS
2827 Seventh Street
Berkeley, CA 94710

Inkworks

Printed on Recycled paper

INTRODUCTION

On my friend's mantelpiece I noticed a small plastic bag filled with sand. It was 1983. I read the label: "Arena de Playa Girón, Bahía de Cochinos, Cuba." Sandy explained that a friend of his had brought it back from an international youth conference. I told him that I had recently read that Columbus walked on that same beach. He cut a corner of the plastic and let the fine white grains trickle into a pyramid on my palm.

Several years before, I had by chance found out about Columbus' role in the genocide of the Taíno Indians. It was revelatory. From that moment, I had a thirst for learning about that era. For me, understanding those earliest events seemed key to understanding all that they had set in motion.

The defeat of the 1961 Bay of Pigs invasion was also a watershed experience in my life. I was twenty years old at the time. My childhood had been dominated by McCarthyism, the Korean war, atomic scares. I was already aware of the CIA's overthrow of progressive governments in Guatemala and the Congo. The Cuban revolution gave me - and many of my generation - a tremendous sense of hope. The Cuban people seemed bent on an independent course of social transformation. But would our North American giant permit a small country to defy it? This was more than a question of Cuba alone: if Cuba could break away from the system, other small countries could too. Perhaps we North Americans who felt oppressed by the same system, perhaps we could break from its oppression too. News of the defeat of the invasion force threw us into a great elation. The euphoria however was short-lived, as the "Cuban missile crisis" began to unfold.

I had not thought about the Bay of Pigs for many years, until I read about Columbus sailing into it. And now this sand. In the intervening period, my understanding of the predatory aspects of the U.S. system had deepened, as had my commitment to work for change.

I brought some sand home. At my desk I sifted the granules back and forth between my palms. And that is how I came to write this history-poem.

The struggle of the Taíno people was not in vain. Today after 500 years the Indian nations are still resisting, although they still suffer daily. The injuries they suffer injure us all. Their struggle to survive is for us all. The indigenous people have never struggled only for physical survival, but for a way of living harmoniously with the planet. The Indian elders are correct when they say that the indigenous people are the caretakers of the world. The grandchildren of colonialism owe the native people an enormous debt. We are still just guests here, and should be humble. Only by joining with the indigenous people in common struggle can non-native people ever hope to become at peace anywhere on this continent and build a constructive future.

John Curl
July 25, 1991

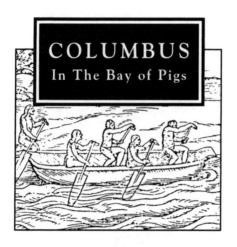

COLUMBUS
In The Bay of Pigs

At home in a caney.
(From Jean de Léry, *Histoire d'un Voyage*, 1527)
(illustration on facing page)

O N E

Yaní tainó, yaní tainó.
Let the Taíno language be heard.
Yaní tainó, yaní tainó. Dayaní.
Goeíz nitaynó guajirós guacá!

Imagine the sand of the beach called
Girón, fine and white, the big bend
that turns the corner of the Bay of Pigs,
Cuba.

Imagina la arena de Playa Girón,
fina y blanca, gira
en el rincón
de la Bahía de Cochinos
Cuba.

Taínos making bread.
(From Girolamo Benzoni, *Historia del Mundo Nuevo*, 1572.)

Tócala. Tómala con la punta de tus dedos.
Déjala caer.
Estás tocando la sangre del imperio.

Touch it. Take some in your fingertips.
Let it fall. You are touching
the blood of empire.

A dark night, April seventeenth, nineteen-
sixty-one: while the U.S. Navy watches,
not far away, fourteen hundred exiles,
recruited in Miami by the CIA,
weapons bulging in every hand,
sail quietly toward the Bahía de Cochinos,
toward the palm-shaded sand of Playa Girón...

A cloudless midday, May twenty-sixth,
fourteen-ninety-four, two years after his first
"voyage of discovery," the Italian Cristoforo
Columbo - Christopher Columbus - called
by the Spaniards Cristóbal Colón - approaches
the mouth of the Bay of Pigs. He is
on his second voyage to "the Indies."
He thinks he is off the coast of China,
and carries letters of state
from the king and queen of Spain
to the Great Emperor Khan.
He stands on the quarterdeck, squinting
at the shore, wondering
if Cuba is finally the mainland he seeks.

Taíno hammocks.
(From Benzoni, 1572)

The sun is a searing disc
directly above his head. His troubled thoughts
turn back to Isabela, his colony on Haiti,
with half his men sick, the rest angry and bitter,
little gold collected, food supplies low,
the Indians strained and wary.

Yesterday's shore had been lined
with Indian villages, the ships
often surrounded by Taíno-Arawaks in canoes
offering songs and gifts to their visitors
from "the sky," (not yet understanding
what it meant
to be subjects of a European king), but today
at the mouth of the Bay of Pigs
Columbus sees no village, the shore
is mangrove swamp, impenetrable.

Suddenly
glistening before them: a white
crescent of sand laced with palm groves.

Churning water: a great herd of beasts!
The Indians call them manatee,
but the seamen call them pigs.

The boats are lowered;
the rowers pull their oars; the hulls
glide through the waves, up onto the beach.
Columbus steps out; his foot sinks
softly into the sand of Playa Girón.

Columbus at Haiti.
(From Columbus' *First Letter*, 1493)

From his log book, these
are his very words:

"At the edge of the sea,
in a great grove of palms
that seemed to reach the sky,
there gushed forth two springs
of water, and when the tide
was on the ebb, the water
was so cold and so sweet
that no better could be found in the world.
No people appeared, but there were signs
of their presence in cut palms.
And we all
rested there on the grass by those springs
among the scent of the flowers
and the sweet singing
of little birds, and all was so gentle,
and the shade of the palms so grand and fair,
to see it all was a wonder!"

So Columbus gushed
over all he found in the Bay of Pigs,
as he did over so much in this New World.
But beneath the enthusiasm
was a dark side of Columbus,
an underside.

Nearby the Bay of Pigs is Laguna de Tesoro,
"Lake of the Treasure," where the local Taínos

Columbus arrives.
(From Columbus' *First Letter*)

threw their sacred objects of gold
to hide them from the Spaniards;
somewhere on the lake bottom
today they are still there.

May twenty-sixth, fourteen-ninety-four;
April seventeenth, nineteen-sixty-one.

Sangre llena las huellas de Cristóbal Colón
en la arena pálida de Playa Girón;
blood fills the footprints of Cristóbal Colón
in the pale sand of Playa Girón.

He hadn't undertaken his "enterprise"
in the spirit of science,
but lusted for gold and power,
and sailed into the setting sun not just
to "discover" the Indies but
to conquer them.

That's the deal he wrangled
from the king and queen of Spain
three years before, that he,
though a commoner, a foreigner, would become
Governor and Viceroy of all
"islands and continents"
that he might "discover and acquire,"
as well as "Admiral of the Ocean Sea," and
be granted "the noble title of *don.*"
And he would get to keep one tenth
of all "gold, silver, pearls, gems, spices,

In the mountains
(From Vespucci, 1509)

and other merchandise" in these lands,
free of all taxes.

But none
of this Columbus was doing for himself
alone. No, he saw visions and portents
and had greater plans: he
had sworn to the Virgin Mary that if she
would guide him by this new route,
bypassing the Moslem blockade
of the road to the East, he would repay her,
within seven years,
by converting the Indies to the Christian Faith,
and by gathering its fabled wealth to pay
for a new crusade
to reconquer the Holy Land from the Infidels.
And the fall of Jerusalem
and recapture of the Holy Sepulchre of
Jesus by his troops, scheduled to occur about
the dawn of the year fifteen-hundred, Columbus
was certain, would be the signal for
the Second Coming.

Sangre llena las huellas de Cristóbal Colón
en la arena pálida de Playa Girón.

And when the Virgin Mary did - or so he
thought - guide Columbus across
the water, at the very first land he touched,
he began to repay her,

Carrying baskets.
(From G.F. de Oviedo y Valdés, *Historia general*, 1547)

by kidnapping six Taínos:

"They interrogated us as if
we had come from heaven," he wrote,
"and cried out in loud voices
to the others, 'Come see the men from the sky.
Bring them food and drink.'
There came many of both sexes, every one
bringing something, giving thanks to God,
prostrating themselves on the earth, lifting up
their hands to heaven... I took by force six
of the Indians from the first island,
and intend to carry them to Spain in order
to learn our language and return, unless your
Highnesses should choose instead to have
them all transported to Spain, or held
captive on the island. These people are
very simple in matters of war... I could
conquer the whole of them with fifty men,
and govern them as I pleased... They are
all of good size and stature, straight-
limbed without exception, and handsomely
formed, with fine shapes and faces; their hair
short, coarse like a horse's tail, combed
toward the forehead except for a small
portion which they let hang down
behind, and never cut... Their eyes are very
large and beautiful... They quickly learn
such words as are spoken to them... They

Domestic scene
(From T. de Bry, *America*, 1594)

*are very clever and honest, display great
liberality, and will give whatever
they possess for a trifle or for nothing
at all... Whether there exists any such thing
as private property among them I have not
been able to ascertain... As they appear
to have no religion, I believe they would very
readily become Christians... They would make
good servants... They are fit to be ordered
about and made to work, to sow, and do
aught else that may be needed, and your
Majesties may build towns and teach
them to go clothed and adopt our customs...
Seeing some with little bits of gold
at their noses, I gathered by signs that by going
southward there would be found a king
with large vessels of gold in large quantities...
To sum up the great profits of this voyage, I am
able to promise, for a trifling assistance
from your Majesties, any quantity of
gold, drugs, cotton, mastic, aloe, and as many
slaves for maritime service as your
Majesties may stand in need of."*

Those are the words of Christopher Columbus.

Yes, Columbus invented the slave trade
in the New World.

*Sangre llena las huellas de Cristóbal Colón
en la arena pálida de Playa Girón.*

The Early Caribbean.   (From Theodore de Bry, *America*, 1594)

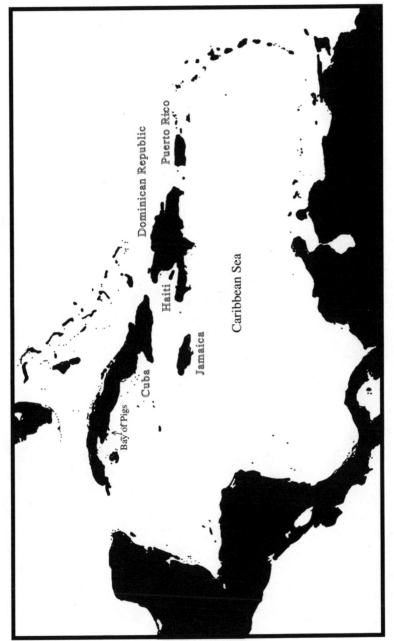

The Caribbean.

Curing the sick.
(From Benzoni, 1574)
(illustration on facing page)

T W O

Who were these Taínos?

Probably the friendliest
people in all the Americas: Taíno means
"peaceful" or "good."

They lived in villages of round
palm-thatched *caneys*, some
with several thousand inhabitants.

The men and boys wore no clothes,
nor did the girls until their first menstruation,
then a small *nagua*, and after marriage
a woven cotton apron. They slept in net
hammocks. The women wore lightning-bugs
in their hair.

Making corn beer.
(From Benzoni, 1574)

Their main weapons
were cane spears with fish-bone tips.
They hunted the groundhog-like hutía
with trained little barkless dogs.
They used pet parrots to decoy wild ones,
then noosed their feet. They braved the sea
in cedar dugout canoes with square ends,
some large enough to carry eighty or more.
They tied a rope to the tail of the remora fish,
and, when the remora attached itself
to another fish by its sucker mouth,
the fisherman would pull them both out.
The Taínos were great swimmers.

Their bread was cassava, baked
on a stone griddle. They kept a pepper-pot soup
simmering at all times. They shaped clay
coils into pots, wove baskets from
biheo leaves. They mixed earth and ashes
into *conuco* mounds where they grew cassava;
near rivers they used ditch irrigation.
On hillsides they planted corn, five kernels
in each hole a pace apart. They grew yams,
beans, pepper, arrowroot, peanuts; kept
orchards of coconuts, papayas, mameys,
pears, annonas, guavas, pineapples.

They had broad flat foreheads, from being
pressed between boards as infants. In their
pierced ears and noses, they wore

Making fire.
(From André Thevet, *Les Singularités*, Paris, 1557.)

shell, bone, stone, and gold.
They painted their bodies
with symbols, the men preferring red,
the women yellow, white, and black.
They bathed daily, using digo root as soap.

To lock a house, they placed a stick
across the entrance, and no Taíno would
think to pass.

Their only rivals were
the Caribs of the Lesser Antilles, who would
raid occasionally in search of women.
The Taínos never raided back.

Who were these Taíno people?

At the hub of each village was a plaza,
a ceremonial center, with a temple housing
the village *zemís*. These were
effigies of stone, wood, shell, or gold, in which
resided messengers to the gods. Near
the temple was a court where they played
a ceremonial ball game in re-creation of a
heroic myth. Close by was the *bohío*, the
large rectilinear home of the *cacique*
and his - or her - extended family.
The cacique's job was the village welfare,
assigning the daily work routine, and
making sure everyone got a fair share. Two
of the main caciques on Haiti when

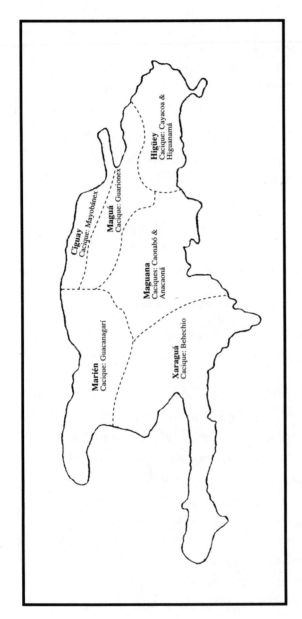

Map of Haiti in Taíno times, with caciques of each province. Today the island that Columbus renamed Española (Hispaniola) houses both the Dominican Republic and modern Haiti.

Ciguay
Cacique: Mayobánex

Maguá
Cacique: Guarionex

Higüey
Cacique: Cayacoa &
Higuanamá

Maguana
Caciques: Caonabó &
Anacaoná

Marién
Cacique: Guacanagarí

Xaraguá
Cacique: Behechio

Columbus arrived were women.

The Taínos danced to *areitos*, songs of tribal
history, of the zemís, of love and mourning.
They danced revolving in circles,
with strings of rattling shells on their wrists
and ankles, waving palm fronds, to the sound
of hollow-log drums, shell timbrels, copper and
gold castanets. The *bohuti*-priests sang areitos
to cure the sick, to the drone of a *maiohavan*,
a wooden gong with a long neck, so resonant
it could be heard a half league away.

Who were these Taíno people?

They believed there is an immortal
being in the sky whom none can see,
who has a mother but no beginning.
They called him Yocahu and his
mother Atabex. The zemís were
their messengers.

They believed that out of a cave called
Yoyovava on the isle of Haiti came
the sun and moon; from two other
nearby caves, Cacibayagua and Amayauba,
came the Taíno people.

They believed that the ocean was formed
from the great flood that poured out
of the stolen calabash

Indian women.
(From Amerigo Vespucci, *Mundus Novus*, Rostok, 1505)

that Dimivan dropped.

They believed that at death their souls
journeyed to the beautiful valley of
Coaybay, presided over by the cacique
Maquetaurié, where they remained
in pleasure forever.

They had a myth - an old story, remembered
in many areitos - of how once a great cacique
named Guamiquiná, who wore
clothes and a beard, came down
from the sky in a ship,
from a place called Turey,
bringing precious gifts and teaching
the Taíno people many skills. Guamiquiná
could only stay a short while, then
left, promising to return someday.

Was it any wonder then, when
Columbus appeared at these same shores,
the Taínos called him Guamiquiná,
expected him to stay only
a short while, and were shocked when
they realized that he didn't plan
to leave at all?

In the zemí-temple was a round wooden table,
on which they kept powdered cohaba-root:
the bohuti-priest would place some
on the head of a zemí, sniff the cohaba

Family portrait.
(From de Léry, 1527)

through a branched cane, fall into a trance,
speak with the zemí, then return with a message
in an archaic tongue. The word *cohaba*
meant "to pray." It was through the cohaba
that the cacique Cacivaquel spoke
with the zemí Yiocavugama, who gave him,
decades prior, a prophesy of the arrival
of the Christians and a warning
of what they would do.
All the caciques knew this prophesy, but hadn't
the heart to tell their people.

Sangre llena las huellas de Cristóbal Colón
en la arena pálida de Playa Girón.

Columbus at Haiti.
(From de Bry, 1594)
(illustration on facing page)

THREE

On his first voyage, two years before
he reached the Bay of Pigs, Columbus wrecked
his flagship *Santa María* on a reef
off Haiti-Bohío-Quisqueya, the cultural center
of the Taíno world. He was rescued
from the reef
by the local chief, Guacanagarí.

Columbus stayed only long enough
to build a fort, then sailed
back to Spain on the *Niña,*
leaving thirty-nine men behind.

Returning ten months later, Columbus found
the settlement burned to the ground.

Guacanagarí had tried to protect the
Christians, but they'd abused the Taíno

Caonabó and Anacaoná
(From de Bry, 1594)

people until Caonabó,
"Golden House," cacique of the golden
mountains of Cibao, the most powerful
chief on Haiti, came down and
killed them all.

Caonabó was held in awe
by the Taínos. By blood half Carib,
the Taínos' only tribal rivals,
he had risen through sheer ability
to the top of the Taíno world.
He shared power with his wife,
Anacaoná, "Flower of Gold,"
renowned for wisdom, graciousness, and
beauty.

Columbus knew
he'd have to settle the score
with Caonabó someday. But first business
was start a new settlement, "Isabela,"
gather gold, and discover the mainland.

So Columbus
left most of his men on Haiti
and sailed off once more,
to the Bay of Pigs and beyond, until
he was so certain
that Cuba was the mainland
that he made his entire crew sign an oath
that they would never say it was an island

Rape of the Taíno Women.
(From de Bry, 1594)

(like the stubborn Indians insisted)
under penalty of having their tongues cut out.

On his return to Haiti,
he found the colony in disastrous straits.
Little gold had been collected, far from enough
to cover expenses, much less fulfill
his extravagant promises.

In desperation
he proposed to the king and queen
(as a temporary expedient of course,
until the gold mines begin to produce),
a plan to capture and sell
all the Carib Indians
on the fanciful grounds
that they were implacable cannibals
and fierce enemies of Spain's friends,
the Taínos.

But the king and queen balked,
as the first few Indians he'd sent quickly died.

Meanwhile, gangs of soldiers were roaming
Haiti, skirting only the province of Caonabó,
committing brutalities of every sort
against the Taínos, who suffered in silence until
one chief, Gua Tiguaná,
ambushed three Spaniards and killed them.
Columbus didn't hesitate:

The Cacique Guarionex leading the Battle of the Vega Real
(From A. de Herrera, *Historia general*, 1601)

by Spanish law, "rebels" could be enslaved; besides,
Taínos were easier to catch than Caribs.
He sent his army to their village, rounded up
fifteen hundred men, women, and children,
chose five hundred fifty of the fittest,
boarded them on four ships, and sent them off
to the slave market in Seville;
the rest Columbus offered to the colonists
as personal slaves, his compliments, no charge.
Two hundred died aboard ship,
and most of the rest soon after arrival.
Gua Tiguaná was condemned to death by arrows,
but chewed through his ropes
and escaped to the mountains,
where he organized resistance.

Columbus found him and attacked
with artillery, cavalry, infantry, and dogs.
In the end, Gua Tiguaná's people
made Columbus another few shiploads of slaves.

Yet he was only a subchief
to the great cacique Caonabó,
who had to be approached now,
but with more caution.

Columbus sent a delegation with gifts
to Caonabó, led
by the intrepid Lt. Ojeda, already famed

Caonabó in chains.
(By Dominican sculptor Abelard Rodriguez Urdaneta)

as the first to enforce Columbus' decree
to cut off the ears or nose of any Indian
stealing Spanish property.

In his village,
high in the mountains of Cibao, Ojeda
met Caonabó, who wore a crown "with wings
on its sides like a shield and golden eyes
as large as silver cups." Ojeda told him
that Columbus offered peace,
if only he would come down
to the settlement to talk. Caonabó, despite
everything, responded, "Yes,
if Guamiquiná wants peace,
I will make peace. I ask only one thing:
to be given
the Christians' church bell as a sign."
So they started down.

Stopping at a river bank, Ojeda held up a
set of manacles to Caonabó, and said,
"These are ceremonial bracelets,
worn only by kings on horseback:
Lord Columbus
has sent them for you to wear
on this great occasion."

So Caonabó became the first Indian
to ever ride
one of these magic creatures called horse.

Punishment for failure to meet tribute payments.
(By de Bry, from B. de las Casas, *Brevissima relación,* Frankfort, 1598.)

Caonabó was tied to the saddle behind Ojeda,
the chains locked on his wrists and ankles;
Ojeda suddenly spurred the horse
across the river, away from the startled
Indian delegation, and hardly stopped until
they reached the settlement, where the greatest
chief of Haiti, instead of being given
the church bell, was thrown at Columbus'
feet, then chained on the porch
of Columbus' house
on the main plaza, for all to see.

The entire island,
except for the village of Guacanagarí,
rose in revolt,
but the Taínos' fish-bone tipped spears
were no match for cold steel,
so all the island was quickly conquered,
and Columbus, imitating Caesar in Gaul,
imposed tribute on the native people.

*Sangre llena las huellas de Cristóbal Colón
en la arena pálida de Playa Girón.*

Each Taíno over fourteen years of age
in the region of Cibao
had to pay enough gold
to fill a hawk's bell measure
every three months, and in return
received a brass token

Taínos pouring molten gold down Spaniards' throats.
(From Benzoni, 1574)

to wear about his neck as proof
of up-to-date payments. Caciques had to pay
a half calabash full of gold
every two months. The penalty
for nonpayment was amputation of the hands.

The gold the Taínos possessed
had been collected over many generations;
within a season Columbus had it all
and the only way the Taínos
could fill their quotas was
to dig it from the river banks. Soon
the streams were filled with whole families,
desperately trying to find enough in time.
They began to flee to the highest mountains
and remotest spots, leaving their crops
unplanted, and famine stalked the land.

But the Christians came after them.
When the Taínos caught a Spaniard now,
they melted gold and poured it down his throat.

Columbus kept the great cacique Caonabó
chained on his front porch for two years, then
put him on a ship for Spain;
he died at sea.

One by one all the chiefs of Haiti,
men and women,
Guarionéx, Behechió, Mayobanéx, Gua Tiguaná,
Cotubanamá, Cayacoá, Higuanamá,

Death of Anacaoná.
(From Las Casas, 1598)

Caonabó's wife Anacaoná,
were tortured, hanged, impaled, burned
at the stake, except for Guacanagarí,
Columbus' one unwavering friend, and he
was banished by his own village, for
Columbus had not exempted even them
from the horrors of the tribute collectors, so
Guacanagarí, an outcast, died
a squalid death on some remote peak.

The Taínos could not understand
why the Christians wanted this gold.

One cacique of Haiti, Hatuey, fled
with his people to Cuba. When told that the
Christians had followed them, he took out
a basket of gold, and said, "Here
is the God of the Christians. They want
us to worship this God: that is why
they struggle with us and kill us. Let us dance
for this God. Who knows? It may please
the Christian God and then they will do us
no harm."

So he and his people danced
before the gold. Then Hatuey hurled
it into the middle of a river.
Not long after,
the Christians caught him
and tied him to a stake. A friar who knew

Death of Hatuey.
(From Las Casas, 1598)

the Taíno language, told Hatuey,
just before they touched the flames,
"If you become a Christian, even now,
you will go to Heaven instead of
to the eternal torment of Hell."

Hatuey asked the friar, "Do
all Christians go to Heaven?" The friar
said, "They do;" and Hatuey replied, "I
would prefer then to go to Hell."

Sangre llena las huellas de Cristóbal Colón
en la arena pálida de Playa Girón.

And so the island of Haiti-Bohío-Quisqueya,
which in Taíno means,
Mountain-House-Of-Which-Nothing-Is-Greater,
a land thriving with millions
of people when Columbus arrived,
within a short time was almost
depopulated.

Most of the Taíno men wound up as slaves
in the mines, most of the women slaves
in the fields, where thousands died
of exhaustion, disease, and hunger.
Those hiding in the mountains saw
that all was lost, and thousands jumped
from cliffs, hanged or stabbed themselves,
or drank cassava poison.

Taínos committing suicide.
(From Benzoni, 1574)

And the beautiful Taíno language
became silence.

Most of the gold, the treasure
of the Taíno nation,
was stowed on a fleet bound for Spain,
but Guabancéx, the zemí of hurricanes,
rose a great wind and sucked the gold
to the ocean bottom, to mix
with the bones of Caonabó.

Faced with a labor shortage, the Christians
sent soldiers to the other islands, to capture
slaves for the mines and plantations
of Haiti, and to begin setting up plantations
and mines on those other islands too.

Sangre llena las huellas de Cristóbal Colón
en la arena pálida de Playa Girón.

This is the Taíno language:

Datoá guariquén ayacavó datiáo.
Mother, come meet my friend.

Mayaní, guaguá areitó ocamá.
Quiet, my baby, listen to the song.

Caconá behiqué chug, darocoél.
Take this gift of medicine, grandfather.

Itá caoná.
I don't have any gold.

Execution of caciques.
(From Las Casas, 1598)

Guaibá cristianós anaquí kanaimá.
Let us get away from the Christian devils.

Baizá! Mayanimacamá!
No! Do not kill me!

Opiá dacá.
I am dead.

Columbus' earliest portrait.
(From Paulus Jovius, *Elogia,* Basel, 1575)
(illustration on facing page)

FOUR

What sort of man was this Columbus?

The son of a weaver, he pretended
to descend from an ancient Roman Consul.

Who was this Columbus?

As an incentive to the sailors on his
first voyage, the king and queen had
offered a reward to the first man
to sight land, a reward of forty thousand
maravedis per year for life: a trifle
for a rich man, a fortune for a poor.

It was a common seaman named
Rodrigo de Triana who was the first
to actually sight and cry, "Land!" but

Torturing a cacique.
(From de Bry, 1594)

when they got back to Spain,
Admiral Columbus claimed
- and got -
the reward himself, for his story of having
seen some beckoning light
in the dark the night before, even though
he never actually cried "Land!" while
the seaman Rodrigo got nothing.

Who was this man Columbus?

He had read the imaginary
Travels of Sir John Mandeville,
and taken it literally, so when he
finally did reach the continent, at
the Orinoco river in Venezuela, Columbus
made perhaps his greatest discovery:

"I have always read that the world
of land and sea is spherical. All authorities
and recorded experiments
have confirmed this until now...
But I have found such great irregularities
here that I have come to the conclusion
that the world is not round,
but the shape of a pear,
with only one side round
and the other jutting out
like a woman's nipple...
I believe that

Enslaved as porters.
(From de Bry, 1594)

the earthly Paradise lies here,
as testified in Holy Scripture,
which no one can enter
except by permission of God."

It was here in Venezuela, on the nipple
of Paradise, that Columbus planned to start
his first mainland colony, in order
to sail upstream to the heights of Eden,
with God's permission, and to harvest
the nearby pearl beds he'd discovered.

Who was this man Columbus?

The Taínos were not the only ones
with reason to hate the Governor:
a steady stream
of colonists returning to Spain
accused him of
abuse of authority, fiscal mismanagement,
withholding of salaries, embezzlement,
boundless personal ambition. Some rose
in the first colonial revolt in the New World,
in alliance with the Taínos,
led by Columbus' former footman and squire,
Francisco Roldán, whom he in his wisdom
had appointed Chief Justice.

Meanwhile almost all the Indian slaves
that Columbus sent to Spain soon died, until
finally the king and queen decided to

Columbus arrested by Bobadilla.
(From de Bry, 1594.)

send the last few Indians alive in Spain
back to the Indies, along with a royal
investigator, Commander Bobadilla, who sailed
into the harbor of Columbus' new capitol,
Santo Domingo, on August twenty-third,
the year fifteen-hundred. The first thing
he saw was three swaying bodies
on the gallows, "rebels"
hanged hours before; the prison held more
"rebels", scheduled for hanging next dawn.

Bobadilla declared Columbus deposed and
ordered him arrested.

But the soldiers who confronted Columbus
suddenly took fright, and none
of them was willing to place the chains
on the Admiral of the Ocean Sea,
until a man stepped forward who knew him
so well he had no fear of him: Espinoza,
Columbus' personal cook, took the
chains from the soldier and snapped them
on his master's wrists.

And so Columbus was sent back to Spain,
to face the mercy of the Crown, and
never fulfilled his vow to the Virgin Mary.

Sugar slaves.
(From de Bry, 1594)
(illustration on facing page)

FIVE

Even with Columbus gone, the mold
had been cast, the conquest and slaughter
on the islands raged on: Haiti, Cuba,
Puerto Rico, Jamaica,
the Antilles, the Bahamas,
millions of Taíno-Arawaks dead,
the entire nation murdered
from the face of the planet, and even then,
the infernos in the mines and plantations
blazed hardly diminished, Taínos
replaced by Caribs, by Aztecs and Mayas
from the mainland, and by slaves
from Africa.

Sangre llena las huellas de Cristóbal Colón
en la arena pálida de Playa Girón.

Gold mine on Haiti.
(From de Bry, 1594)

It was only the slave trade with Europe
that the king and queen saw fit to ban.
"Rebels" could still be enslaved, but had to be
kept in the Indies. When a Spaniard
was granted land, he was also "granted "
all the Indians living on that land, as serfs:
this was the *encomienda* system
used to subdue all Spanish America.

And so the Caribbean of today
was slowly formed. As the native
people changed into the present
mixed population, so the yoke
of Spain was replaced by North
American domination. Yet the Caribbean
people still found themselves
impoverished and enslaved.

Meanwhile on the northern continent,
from the earliest years
when the New England Puritans
waged genocidal war
on the Narragansett Indian alliance,
through the 1890 massacre of Lakota families
at Wounded Knee,
the Anglo-American invaders
wanted only the land, not the people,
and removed the northern Indian nations from it
by any means necessary.
The Bureau of Indian Affairs, formed in

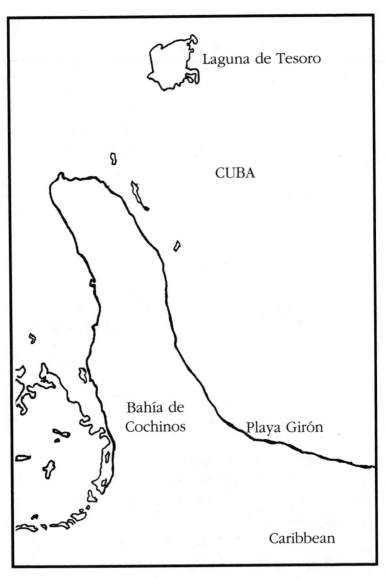

The Bay of Pigs.

the Department of War, was moved
to the Department of "the Interior"
to consolidate the conquest,
and they no longer recognized
the North American Indians as citizens
of independent nations.

But the U. S. A. was still hungry
for further domination, so turned south, and
by 1954 staged over 55 armed interventions
in Latin America.

In Cuba, 1958, foreigners
owned and controlled
seventy-five percent of all arable land;
the police chief of Havana received
$730,000 dollars per month
from the gambling casinos,
while the new native people,
the campesinos,
did not eat regularly.

But now the Cuban people had more than
fish-bone tipped spears to fight back with.

December 1958:
the revolutionary guerrillas
of the 26th of July Movement descend
from the Sierra Maestra mountains
and fight their way toward the cities.

Attack on a village.
(From de Bry, 1594)

The U.S. client dictator flees; the streets
fill with dancers.

For the next two years, Cuba struggles
toward independence from all
foreign domination and social prosperity
for its working population.

But the U.S. of North America
declares a general embargo on Cuba,
forbids its citizens to travel to Cuba,
breaks diplomatic relations with Cuba.

A dark night, April 17, 1961:
while the U.S. Navy watches,
not far away, fourteen hundred exiles,
recruited in Miami by the CIA,
sail quietly toward the mouth
of the Bahía de Cochinos,
the Bay of Pigs, weapons bulging in every hand,
and in their crosshairs, the young
Cuban revolutionaries, for their crime
of overthrowing a brutal regime
and their sin
of trying to break the stranglehold of
the almighty dollar.
While on the beach, between the palms,
on the fine white sand of Playa Girón,
by chance, a jeep drives up,
and two Revolutionary Militiamen,

Carib resistance.
(From Plautius, *Nova Typis Transacta Navagatio,* 1621)

sensing something wrong, stop and
shine their headlights into the face
of the oncoming waves...

Toca la arena. Tómala con la punta de tus dedos.
Déjala caer. Estás tocando
la sangre del imperio.

Touch the sand. Take some in your fingertips.
Let it fall. You are touching
the blood of empire.

May twenty-sixth, fourteen-ninety-four;
April seventeenth, nineteen-sixty-one:

Sangre llena las huellas de Cristóbal Colón
en la arena pálida de Playa Girón.

Datoá, guariquén ayacavó datiaó.
Mother, come meet my friend.

Mayaní, guaguá, areitó ocamá.
Quiet, my baby, listen to the song.

Caconá behiqué chug, darocoél.
Take this gift of medicine, grandfather.
Dayaní.
I will speak.

Goeíz nitaynó guajirós guacá.
The Taíno people live!

Taíno canoe.
(From Oviedo, 1547)

Yaní tainó, yaní tainó.
Let the Taíno language be heard.
Let the Taíno language be heard.

Yaní tainó, yaní tainó. Dayaní.
Goeíz nitaynó guajirós guacá!

SELECTED BIBLIOGRAPHY

RECOMMENDED READING

Galeano, Eduardo, *Genesis: Memories of Fire,* NY,1988.

Irving, Washington, *The Life and Voyages of Columbus,* 1827.

Koning, Hans, *Columbus: His Enterprise,* New York, 1976.

Olsen, Fred, *On the Trail of the Arawaks,* Norman, 1974.

Sale, Kirpatrick, *The Conquest of Paradise,* NY, 1990.

Small, Deborah, and Maggie Jaffe, *1492,* Warren College, 1990.

Taylor, Douglas, *Languages of the West Indies,* Baltimore, 1977.

Williams, Eric, *From Columbus to Castro,* New York, 1970.

ORIGINAL SOURCES

Anghiera, Pietro Martire d', *The Decades of Peter Martyr* (*De Orbe Novo,* 1516), New York, 1912.

Bernáldez, Andrés, *Historia de los Reyes Católicos* (c1498), Sevilla, 1856, in *Voyages of Columbus,* London,1930.

Casas, Bartolome de las, *History of the Indies (Historia de las Indias,* c.1575); Mexico, 1951, New York, 1971; *The Devastation of the Indies,* (1552) New York, 1974.

Columbus, Christopher, *The Diario of Columbus' First Voyage,* (1492), Norman, Oklahoma, 1989; *The Four Voyages,* Baltimore, 1969.

Columbus, Ferdinand, *The Life of the Admiral Christopher Columbus by his Son Ferdinand,* (1571), New Brunswick, 1959.

Cuneo, Michele de, Letter on the Second Voyage, (1496) in Morison, S.E., *Journals and other Documents on Christopher Columbus,* New York, 1963.